World Languages

Colors in Italian

Daniel Nunn

Chicago, Illinois

www.capstonepub.com
Visit our website to find out more information about Heinemann-Raintree books.

To order:
☎ Phone 800-747-4992
💻 Visit www.capstonepub.com to browse our catalog and order online.

© 2013 Heinemann Library
an imprint of Capstone Global Library, LLC
Chicago, Illinois

Edited by Rebecca Rissman, Dan Nunn, and Sian Smith
Designed by Joanna Hinton-Malivoire
Picture research by Elizabeth Alexander
Production by Alison Parsons
Originated by Capstone Global Library Ltd
Printed and bound in China by South China Printing Company Ltd

16 15 14 13 12
10 9 8 7 6 5 4 3 2 1

Library of Congress Cataloging-in-Publication Data
Nunn, Daniel.
  Colors in Italian : i colori / Daniel Nunn.
    p. cm.—(World languages - Colors)
  Includes bibliographical references and index.
  ISBN 978-1-4329-6655-3—ISBN 978-1-4329-6662-1 (pbk.)
1. Italian language—Textbooks for foreign speakers—English—Juvenile literature. 2. Colors—Juvenile literature. I. Title.
  PC1129.E5N86 2013
  458.2'421—dc23   2011046688

Acknowledgments
We would like to thank Shutterstock for permission to reproduce photographs: pp.4 (© Phiseksit), 5 (© Stephen Aaron Rees), 6 (© Tischenko Irina), 7 (© Tony Magdaraog), 8 (© szefei), 9 (© Picsfive), 10 (© Eric Isselée), 11 (© Yasonya), 12 (© Nadezhda Bolotina), 13 (© Maryna Gviazdovska), 14 (© Erik Lam), 15 (© Eric Isselée), 16 (© Ruth Black), 17 (© blueskies9), 18 (© Alexander Dashewsky), 19 (© Michele Perbellini), 20 (© Eric Isselée), 21 (© Roman Rvachov).

Cover photographs reproduced with permission of Shutterstock: dog (© Erik Lam), strawberry (© Stephen Aaron Rees), fish (© Tischenko Irina). Back cover photograph of a cake reproduced with permission of Shutterstock (© Ruth Black).

We would like to thank Nino Puma for his invaluable assistance in the preparation of this book.

Every effort has been made to contact copyright holders of material reproduced in this book. Any omissions will be rectified in subsequent printings if notice is given to the publisher.

Contents

Rosso

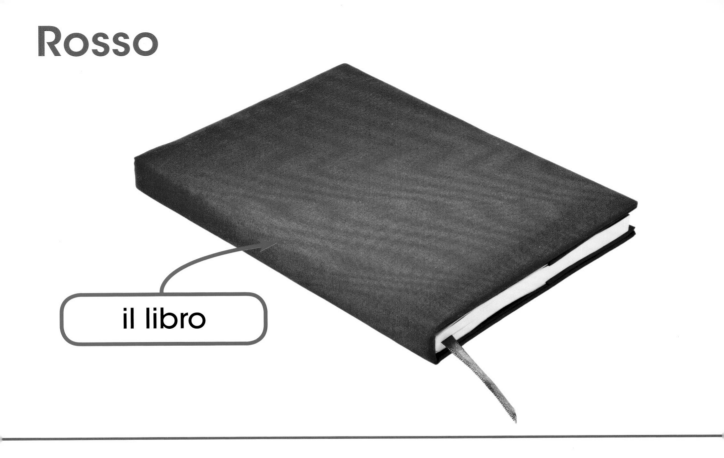

il libro

Il libro è rosso.

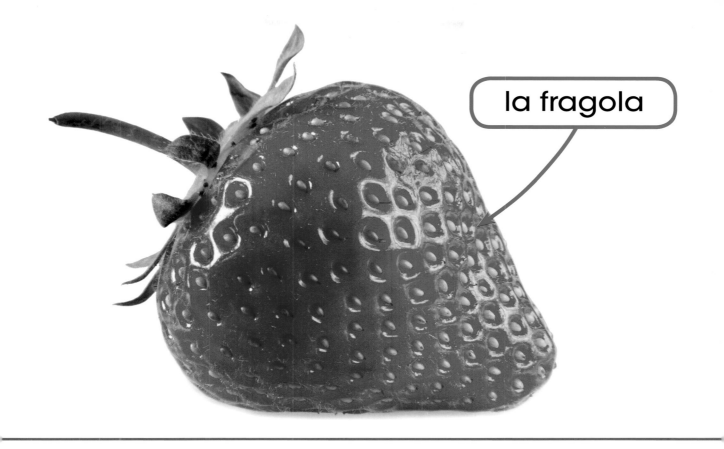

la fragola

La fragola è rossa.

Arancione

il pesce

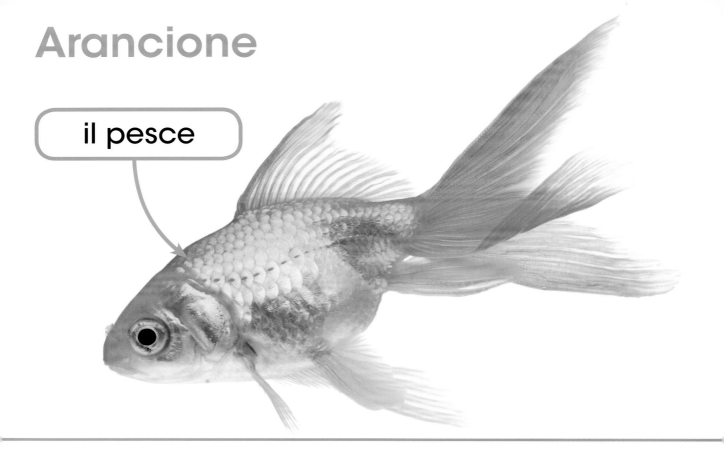

Il pesce è arancione.

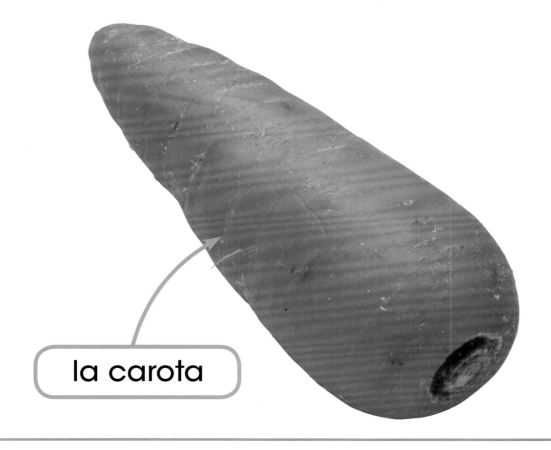

la carota

La carota è arancione.

Giallo

il fiore

Il fiore è giallo.

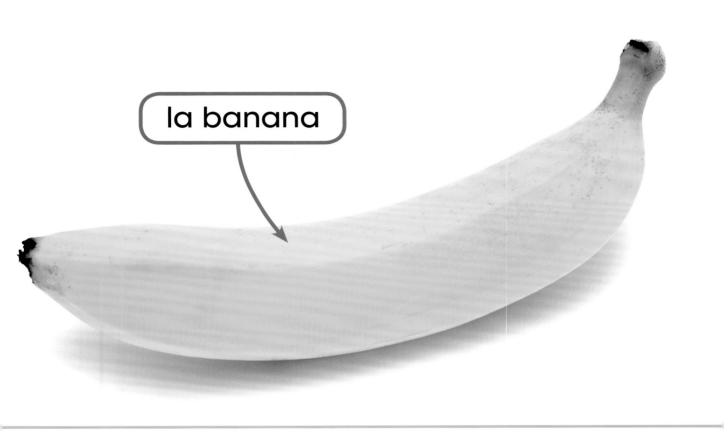

la banana

La banana è gialla.

Verde

l'uccello

L'uccello è verde.

la mela

La mela è verde.

Blu

la maglietta

La maglietta è blu.

la tazza

La tazza è blu.

Marrone

il cane

Il cane è marrone.

la mucca

La mucca è marrone.

Rosa

il pasticcino

Il pasticcino è rosa.

il cappello

Il cappello è rosa.

Bianco

il latte

Il latte è bianco.

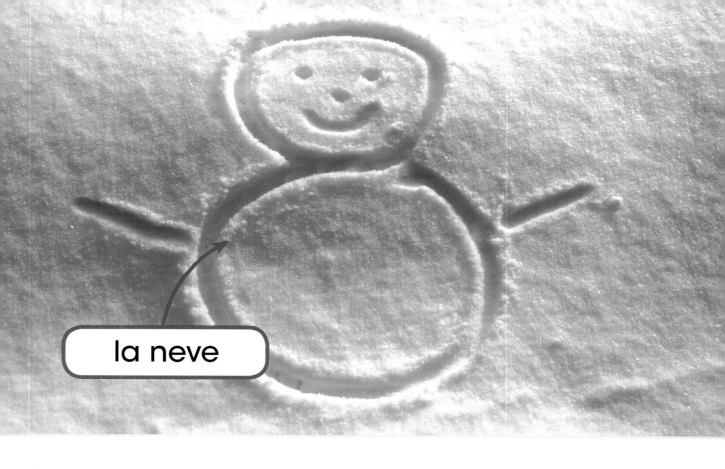

la neve

La neve è bianca.

Nero

Il gatto è **nero**.

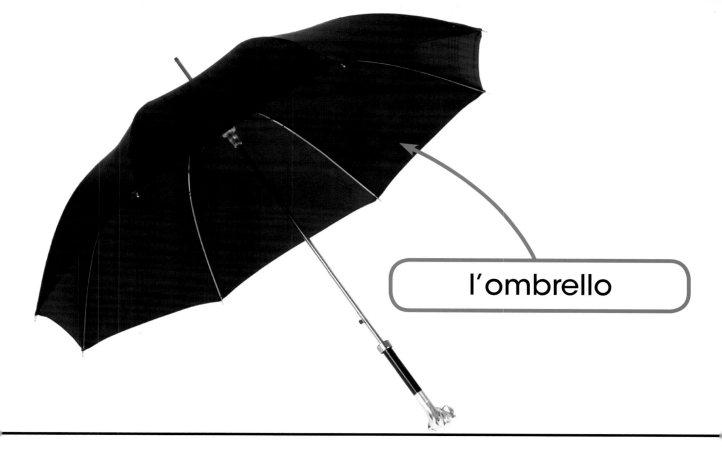

l'ombrello

L'ombrello è **nero**.

Dictionary

Italian Word	How To Say It	English Word
arancione	ar-ran-choh-nay	orange
banana	baa-naa-naa	banana
bianca/bianco	be-an-kah/be-an-koh	white
blu	bloo	blue
cane	ka-nay	dog
cappello	kap-pel-loh	hat
carota	kar-rot-ta	carrot
è	eh	is
fiore	fee-oar-ay	flower
fragola	fragg-o-lah	strawberry
gatto	gat-toh	cat
gialla / giallo	jal-la / jal-loh	yellow
il	eel	the (masculine)
la	lah	the (feminine)
latte	lat-tay	milk
libro	lee-broh	book

Italian Word	How To Say It	English Word
maglietta	mah-lee-ay-tah	T-shirt
marrone	mar-roh-nay	brown
mela	meh-lah	apple
mucca	moo-kah	cow
nero	nare-oh	black
neve	nay-vay	snow
ombrello	ohm-brey-loh	umbrella
pasticcino	pa-stee-chee-noh	cake
pesce	peh-shay	fish
rosa	roh-sa	pink
rossa / rosso	ros-sa / ros-so	red
tazza	tah-tsa	cup
uccello	oo-chel-loh	bird
verde	vair-day	green

See words in the "How To Say It" columns for a rough guide to pronunciations.

23

Index

Notes for Parents and Teachers

In Italian, nouns are either masculine or feminine. The word for "the" changes accordingly—either il (masculine) or la (feminine). Sometimes adjectives have different spellings too, depending on whether the noun is masculine or feminine. This is why some of the colors have more than one spelling.

24